To Aidan Gilliland
From Alex W

Following the death of his grandad (Grandans as Alexander called him) at the age of 57 to pancreatic cancer, and his own intensive chemotherapy for Acute Lymphoblastic Leukaemia, Alexander wrote down this story which touched our hearts. I hope you love its simplicity.

Alexander is now 13 and growing stronger day by day.

Copyright © 2011 – Alexander Warne

First published in Great Britain by Canaan Press in 2011

Canaan Press
PO Box 3070
Littlehampton
West Sussex
BN17 6WX
office@canaanpress.co.uk
www.canaanpress.co.uk

The book imprint of
Matt's Canaan Trust
www.mattscanaantrust.com

All rights reserved. No part of this publication may be reproduced,
stored in a retrieval system, or transmitted in any form or by any means – for example,
electronic, photocopy, recording – without prior written permission of the publisher.
The only exception is brief quotations in printed and broadcasted reviews.

British Library Cataloguing in Publication Data
A record of this book is available from the British Library

ISBN: 978-1-907505-06-5

Book design by Andy Ashdown Design
www.andyashdowndesign.co.uk

Illustrations by Nadia Chalk and Alexander Warne

Manufactured in Malta by Gutenberg Press Limited

The Heaven Flower

Alexander Warne

Aged 7

*Dedicated to the memory of
Patrick Brian Gratwick (Paddy) –
a loving and fun grandad.*

One day in a great meadow, Alexander was walking through the grass when suddenly he saw a beautiful plant rising from the ground.

He had never seen such a perfect flower.

Alexander decided to take it back to his mum so that she could make a home for it in their garden.

The flower looked as though it had been planted by God or some kind of Angel.

The next day, the flower had grown a lot.

Mum was busy looking after it while Alexander played with his cat, Charlie.

Alexander's nan sat watching him with Charlie, and she enjoyed the sun.

That night while Alexander was in bed, he suddenly saw some kind of glowing outside his window.

He sat up with astonishment, put on his dressing gown, and rushed outside to see where the strange light was coming from.

In the garden, Alexander saw sparks of light shooting from the meadow flower. He reached out his hand and grabbed one of the stars.

All at once, another sort of glow came from the flower – but this was an *extraordinary* glow.

Then Alexander heard a voice …

It was a voice he knew.

A whirlpool of light appeared –
and Alexander saw his Grandans.

Grandans wanted to take Alexander on a magical journey in his amazing flying car.

Alexander quickly gathered up his portable games console and penknife, and everything he'd kept that belonged to Grandans.

Then they climbed into the flying car and took off through the air …

They flew over swamps, villages and zoos.

They landed at one particular zoo where they saw snakes, lions, hippos, and Alexander's favourites – the monkeys and rats.

A rat called Eric was the one Alexander loved best. He and Grandans went to talk to Eric.

Then Alexander opened the cage to the snakes. Grandans wasn't too keen on snakes so he stood back.

Grandans opened up a little box that contained an Angel.

'This is my Guardian Angel,' Grandans said.

'But I thought *you* were an Angel,' said Alexander.

'That's true, I am,' replied Grandans. 'But Angels have to have Guardian Angels as well.'

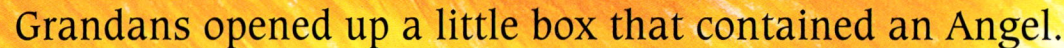

Suddenly, Grandans' Guardian Angel started to whirl round and round, and showed Alexander something wonderful – first, what had happened to him in his past. Then, what was going to happen to him in his future!

'In your future, Alexander,'
said Grandans' Guardian Angel,
'you will have a loving family and a wonderful life.'

Alexander climbed back out of the Pacific Ocean into the flying car with Grandans helping him.

Alexander was soaking wet, but the car was warm and dry and soon they were off again.

Can you guess where Alexander and Grandans are going next?

Write your answer here

....

They spoke to sharks, whales, dolphins and all kinds of fish.

Grandans took Alexander way up into the sky. Alexander asked him where they were going.

'It's a surprise, Alexander,' said Grandans. 'But I'll tell you this. We're already there!'

Alexander was now at the stairs to Heaven.

He and Grandans walked up the stairs to the Golden Gates that shone like the sun.

Was your guess right?   Yes / No

Alexander said, 'Where are we Grandans? How did we get here? All I saw was a flash of light.'

'We are in Heaven, where my home is,' replied Grandans. 'My friends are waiting for us.'

Alexander saw two of Grandans' friends. They were girls.
But there was a boy there, too.

The boy was God.

'No humans are allowed up here,' said God.

'But Alexander is my grandson,' answered Grandans.

'In that case,' said God, 'give him a tour of Heaven. Then, I'm afraid he must go.'

Grandans took Alexander into different rooms that were special to God.

Alexander saw the Crystal Healing Room, the Star Room, the Angel Room and the Garden Room.

Grandans looked after the Garden Room.

With a heavy heart, Grandans told Alexander it was time to go.

Alexander didn't feel sad. He felt happy because he knew that Grandans was happy and didn't have any more pain. Now Grandans looked the way he did before he was ill.

Stars started flashing – then suddenly it was dark again …

The next morning, Alexander was woken by his mum.
He rubbed his eyes and thought about his magical
journey with Grandans in the flying car.

Had it all been just a dream?

But then Alexander opened his hand.

Inside was a small piece of paper. He unfolded it to find a note from his Grandans!

Alexander read it once slowly. Then he read it once more, just to make sure.

'When you want to see me again,' Grandans had written, 'just close your eyes and believe.'

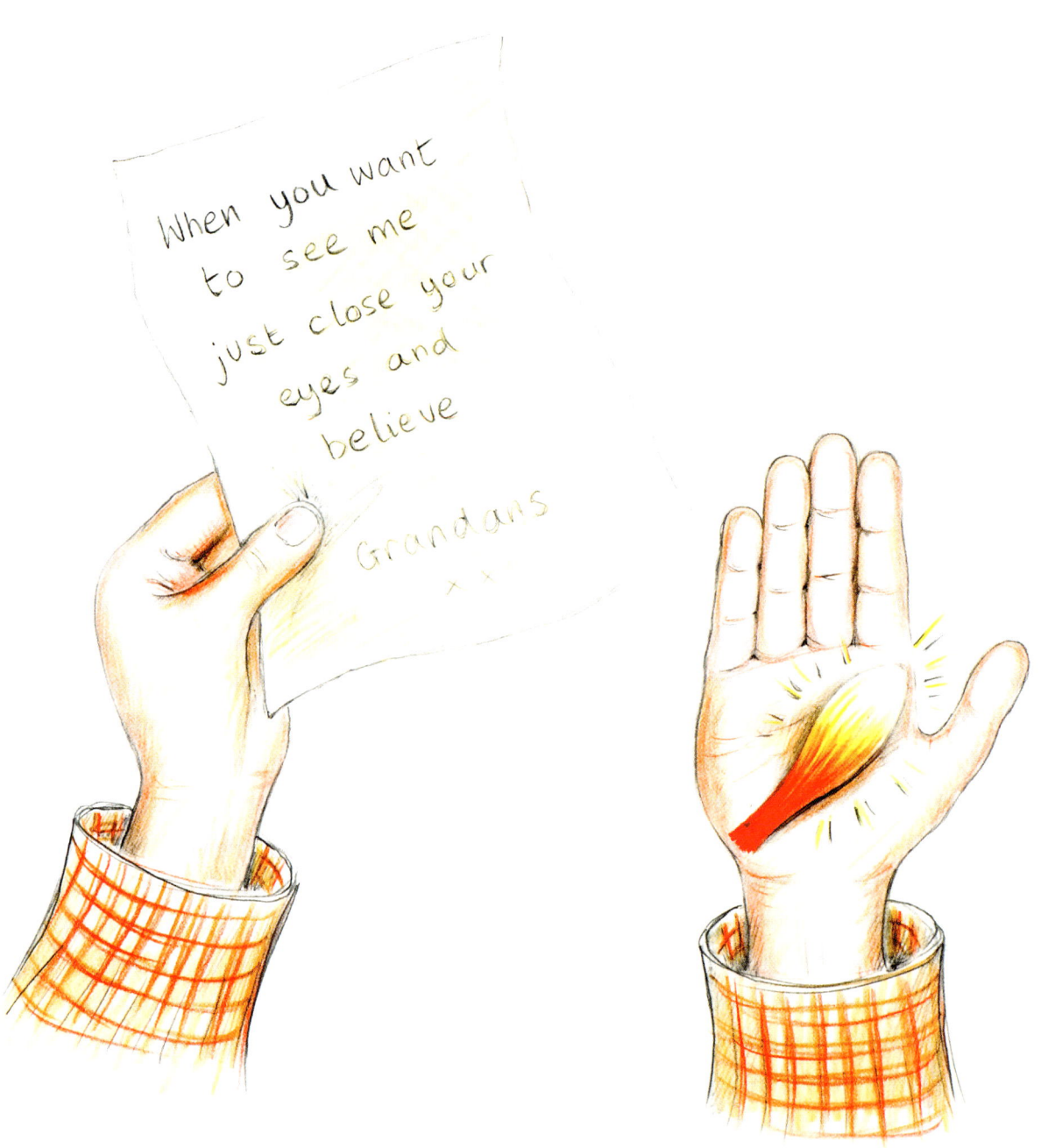

Alexander smiled.

He read the note to his mum. She listened carefully.

Then Alexander's mum smiled, too.

Why I wrote the story

The reasons I wrote *The Heaven Flower* are because when someone you love dies, you feel alone. This book shows that you are not alone and that it happens to everyone in some stage in their life. The moral of this story is that nobody really dies as long as you still love them. Going through cancer is like a living hell and my grandad was the closest person to me apart from my mum and dad. When he died I experienced things I could not explain and saw him all the time.

Story behind the story

At the age of 6 I experienced three bad things that happened within a few weeks of each other. First my mum had a miscarriage on the 8 November 2003. On the 16 December I was diagnosed with Acute Lymphoblastic Leukaemia and then my grandad was diagnosed with cancer of the pancreas at the beginning of January and died on the 16 May 2004 – the day after my 7th birthday. The day after my grandad's funeral, I wrote this book from an experience that I believed really happened. I was 7 years old when I wrote this.

Alexander Warne